BELWIN MASTER

SAXOPHONE ADV

GRADED SOLOS for the Developing Musician
Composed or Arranged by KEITH SNELL

Volume 2

CONTENTS

Design: Odalis Soto

ORIENTATION

This book is the third of three folios of saxophone duets in the Belwin Master Duets, Volume 2, series. As with the Belwin Master Duets, Volume 1, each of these folios contains a collection of graded duets that should prove to be a useful resource for both the student and the teacher of the saxophone.

Each folio contains transcriptions of works from all periods of music history, arrangements of folk songs and traditional tunes, plus a selection of original compositions by the editor. These duets will challenge the advanced student in rhythm, range, and key signatures in music that is both instructive and enjoyable to perform. The teacher will find these duets useful because each has been carefully arranged to develop the student's overall instrumental technique and musicianship.

ADVANCED LEVEL - DUETS

The duets in this folio are designed to provide the advanced level saxophone student with the greatest challenges in all areas of playing. As with the Intermediate level Master Duets, special emphasis has been placed on exposing the student to a wide range of musical styles from all periods of history. However, much more attention is given to the use of phrase marks, dynamic markings, articulation and ornaments. It is hoped that these saxophone duets will provide new challenges to the advanced student while encouraging a broader interest in the many styles of music.

Capriccio

George Frideric Handel (1685-1759)

4

Serenade

Keith Snell

7

Two-Part Invention No. 14

Johann Sebastian Bach (1685-1750)

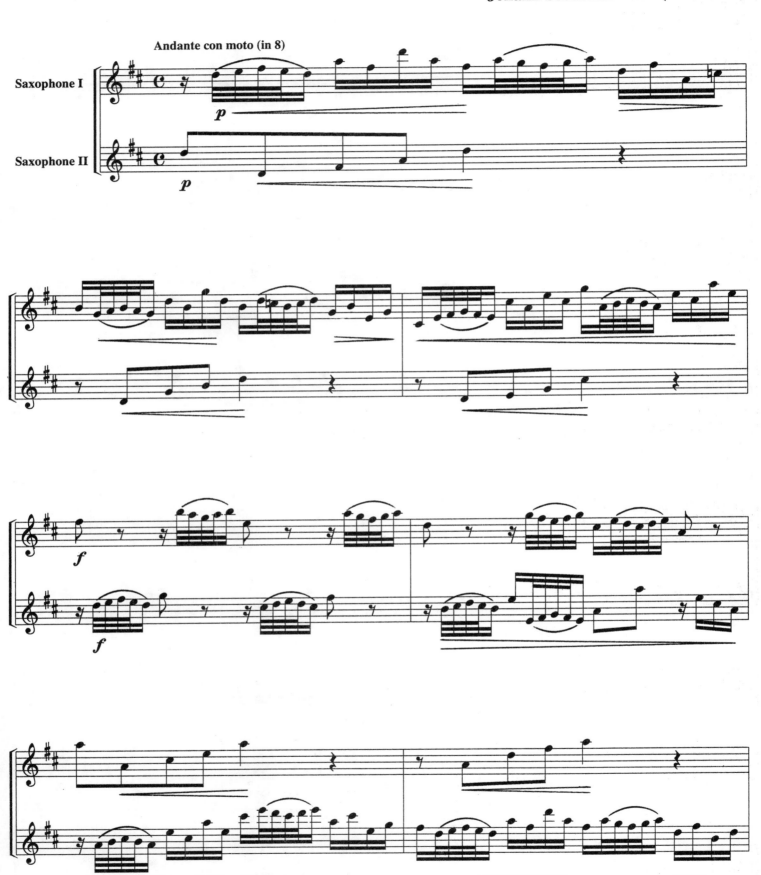

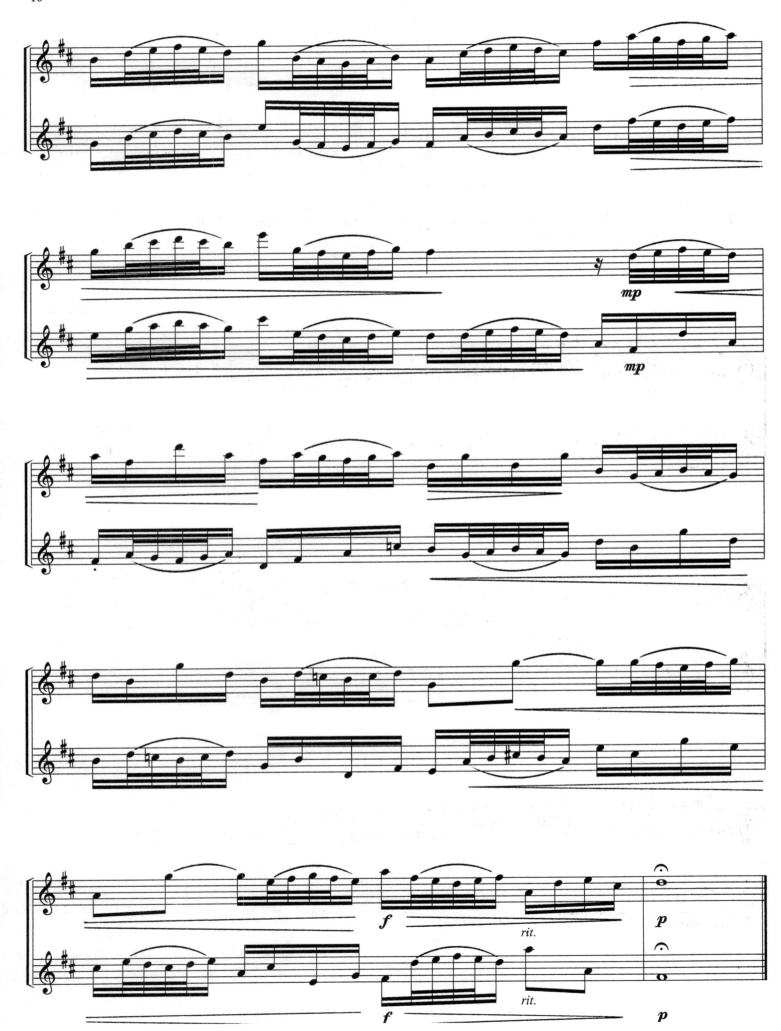

Parallels

Keith Snell